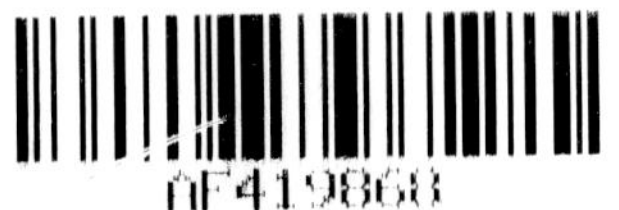

The Sigil of Eternal Spirals journal

The Sigil of Eternal Spirals journal

Matthew Petchinsky

CONTENTS

The Sigil of Eternal Spirals journal
By: Matthew Petchinsky